I0458089

FINDING MEANING

BETWEEN

MATTER AND MIND

Hakim Ibn Adam

Centre for Studies in Matter, Mind, and Meaning

threerosespublishing.com

ISBN: 978-1-9990656-8-3

DEDICATION

To all seekers who dare to wonder what reality is, and
who never stop asking how they fit within it.

Contents

INTRODUCTION

You know that you're conscious.

"Whatever else" you might doubt; whether the external world really exists, whether your memories are accurate, whether other people have minds like yours.

But you can't doubt that: you're experiencing something right now.

There's a felt quality to reading these words, to sitting where you're sitting, to thinking the thoughts you're thinking. This undeniable reality of experience, this consciousness, is the one certainty you have.

But consciousness creates a puzzle. You seem to exist in a physical world—a world of matter and energy, of atoms and molecules, of brains and bodies. This physical world appears to follow precise mathematical laws that have nothing to say about consciousness, about experience, about what anything feels like. Physics describes particles and forces. Chemistry describes molecular interactions. Neuroscience describes brain activity. But none of these descriptions seems to capture the felt reality of being conscious.

So, what's the relationship between consciousness and the physical world? How does your inner life of thoughts and feelings connect to the outer world of matter and energy? How does the experience of seeing red relate to the physical processes in your brain? How does the sensation of pain connect to the firing of neurons?

This isn't just an abstract philosophical puzzle. How you answer this question shapes everything else: how you understand yourself, how you think about other people, how you relate to nature, what you think knowledge is, whether you believe your choices matter, and what makes life meaningful.

THE USUAL ANSWERS DON'T WORK

For most of modern history, the dominant answer has been *materialism*: consciousness somehow emerges from purely physical processes. According to this view, the brain is essentially a biological computer, and consciousness is what computation feels like from the inside.

It sounds scientific and hard-headed.

The problem is that it doesn't actually explain

anything. How do unconscious particles, following physical laws with no reference to experience, suddenly produce experience? At what point does the light of consciousness switch on? And why?

Some people go the opposite direction: maybe consciousness is all there is, and the physical world is somehow dependent on the mind. This view—*idealism*—has ancient roots and sophisticated defenders. But it creates its own problems. If everything is mental, why is the world so stable and law-governed? Why do we all experience the same reality? Why does mathematics work so well for predicting physical events?

We're stuck. Materialism can't explain consciousness. Idealism can't explain the physical world. Both views start by assuming that reality must be fundamentally one kind of thing—either unconscious matter or conscious mind—and then struggle to explain how the other appears.

What if the problem isn't that we haven't found the right answer? What if the problem is the question itself—the assumption that we have to choose between mind and matter, between consciousness and the physical world?

A DIFFERENT STARTING POINT

This book articulates a different approach. Instead of starting with matter or mind, we'll start with something more fundamental: *process*. Instead of asking whether reality is made of unconscious stuff or conscious experience, we'll recognize that reality is ongoing activity, continuous happening, creative advance.

And here's the key insight: processes aren't purely physical or purely mental. They have both an exterior aspect—what we can observe and measure from outside—and an interior aspect—what it's like, however minimally, to be that process. Physical description and experiential description aren't competing accounts of reality. They're two perspectives on the same reality, neither complete without the other.

This isn't just philosophical speculation. It emerges from taking seriously what physics, biology, and our own experience actually show us. Physics reveals that observation affects what's observed, that particles are better understood as processes than as things, and that relationships are fundamental. Biology shows us that organisms aren't separate from their environments but are constituted by their relationships. And our own consciousness shows us that knowing isn't passive reception but active participation.

When we put these insights together, we get a picture of reality that's radically different from common sense but also more coherent. Consciousness isn't a mysterious addition to an otherwise unconscious universe. It's a sophisticated development of something fundamental to reality itself—the interior, experiential aspect of process. And matter isn't dead stuff that somehow gives rise to consciousness. It's the exterior, structural aspect of the same processes that have experience as their interior character.

WHAT THIS BOOK WILL DO

This book will build this understanding systematically, step by step. We'll start by examining why the usual views—materialism and idealism—create unsolvable puzzles. Then we'll develop an alternative through four key insights:

First, reality is better understood as process than as things. Everything is happening, becoming, changing. What we call objects are stable patterns in an ongoing process.

Second, processes have an interior character—some form of experience, however minimal. Not human-like consciousness all the way down, but responsiveness, taking-account-of, being-affected-by. Experience varies enormously in complexity, but it's present in some form at every level.

Third, processes are fundamentally relational. Nothing exists in isolation. What something *is* depends on what it's connected to. Relationships aren't optional—they're constitutive.

Fourth, knowing is participatory. You don't passively observe an independent reality. You actively participate in reality through the relationships you establish with it. What you know depends partly on how you know it.

These four insights work together to give us a

unified picture where consciousness and matter are aspects of one reality, where mind and body aren't separate realms but different perspectives on the same processes, and where knowing is participation rather than observation.

WHO THIS BOOK IS FOR

This book is for anyone puzzled by consciousness and its place in nature. You don't need a background in philosophy or science. The ideas are explained from the ground up, using everyday examples rather than technical jargon. The goal is clarity, not comprehensiveness. We're not surveying every possible view or engaging with every academic debate. We're building one coherent way of understanding reality that solves the puzzles without creating new ones.

If you've ever wondered how your inner life of thoughts and feelings relates to your physical brain... if you've felt the strangeness of being a conscious being in a seemingly unconscious universe... if you want to understand yourself and your place in reality more deeply... this book is for you.

The view we'll develop might seem strange at first. It requires letting go of some deeply ingrained assumptions—that things are more fundamental than processes, that consciousness is rare and special, that knowing is passive observation.

But if you're willing to follow the argument, you'll

find that this strangeness dissolves into a more natural way of understanding reality—one where consciousness fits seamlessly into nature, where you're not alienated from the world but participating in it, where both scientific investigation and direct experience reveal genuine aspects of one unified reality.

THE INVITATION

Philosophy at its best isn't just about understanding—it's about living differently in light of understanding. If this view makes sense, it changes how you experience consciousness, how you relate to others, how you engage with nature, how you think about your choices and your life.

That transformation is the real goal. Understanding is valuable, but only if it helps you inhabit reality more fully, more consciously, more authentically. The puzzles about consciousness and matter aren't just intellectual exercises. They're questions about your place in reality, about what you are and how you're connected to everything else.

So, let's begin. Not with final answers—deep mysteries will remain—but with sufficient clarity to dissolve the false puzzles, to make sense of experience, and to live well in light of understanding.

We'll start where the problems are most obvious: with the common-sense view that reality is made of unconscious stuff, and the deep puzzles that follow.

The Problem with Matter

We all grow up with a particular way of thinking about the world. It seems so obvious that we rarely question it: the world is made of things—solid, definite objects that exist whether we're looking at them or not. Tables, chairs, rocks, trees, planets, atoms. These things have properties—color, weight, shape, position—and they interact with each other according to rules we can discover. Your coffee cup sits on the table. The table supports the cup. Both are made of molecules, which are made of atoms, which are made of smaller particles still. This picture of reality is so ingrained that it feels like simple common sense.

And for most everyday purposes, this way of thinking works perfectly well. Engineers build bridges that don't fall down. Doctors prescribe medicines that cure diseases. Astronomers predict eclipses centuries in advance. All of this practical success seems to confirm our basic intuition: reality is fundamentally made of stuff, arranged in various ways, and following discoverable laws.

But when we look more carefully—especially at the edges where consciousness meets the physical world—this common-sense picture starts to break down in strange and troubling ways. It's not that the picture is completely wrong. It's that it's incomplete in ways that matter deeply, and these incompleteness problems aren't minor puzzles waiting for better technology. They are fundamental gaps in how we're thinking about reality itself.

Let's look at three of these problems. None of them requires advanced physics or philosophy to understand. They're puzzles that emerge directly from taking our common-sense view seriously and pushing it to see what it actually implies.

THE MEASUREMENT PROBLEM

Here's something genuinely odd about the world, something discovered through careful experiments rather than philosophy: the act of observing something can change what that thing is doing.

This isn't like checking your tire pressure and letting out a little air in the process. That's a measurement effect we can account for—the measuring disturbs the system in predictable, mechanical ways. What physicists discovered in the quantum realm is far stranger: before you measure a particle's position, it doesn't have a definite position. It exists in a kind of blurred state, spread across multiple possible locations. The act of measurement doesn't just reveal where it was—it makes it *be* somewhere specific.

Imagine if checking your bank account didn't just tell you the balance but actually determined what the balance would be. That is the kind of weirdness we are dealing with, except it's not a thought experiment—it's how the subatomic world actually behaves.

Now, if the world is fundamentally made of unconscious stuff, following mechanical rules with no reference to consciousness, this makes no sense whatsoever. Why should particles "care" whether they are being observed? What even counts as observation?

The standard response is to say this is just a mystery we haven't solved yet, a feature of quantum mechanics we don't fully understand. And that is fair enough. But notice what we're doing: we're encountering a situation where consciousness and matter seem deeply entangled, where the act of knowing affects what is known, and we're treating this as a temporary anomaly rather than a clue about something fundamental.

What if the weirdness isn't a bug in our understanding—what if it's pointing to something wrong with the basic picture?

THE COMBINATION PROBLEM

Here's another puzzle. According to our common-sense view, the fundamental building blocks of reality are unconscious. Electrons don't feel anything. Quarks have no inner life. Atoms don't experience. They just *are*—moving and interacting according to physical laws, but with no awareness, no sensation, nothing *it's like to be them.*

Yet here we are: conscious, aware, experiencing. You're reading these words right now. There's something *it feels like to be* you at this moment— perhaps you're comfortable or uncomfortable, focused or distracted, interested or skeptical. This felt quality of experience, this consciousness, is the most undeniable thing in your life. Even if you doubt everything else, you can't doubt that you're experiencing doubt.

So, the question becomes: if the fundamental ingredients are completely unconscious, and consciousness emerges only when you arrange these unconscious ingredients in sufficiently complex patterns (like brains), how exactly does that work?

It's not enough to say "complexity produces consciousness." Complexity is just having lots of parts doing lots of things. Your liver is enormously complex, but there's nothing *it's like to be* your liver. A city is complex, but cities don't have unified experiences. A computer running a simulation of a brain is complex, but we don't typically think the computer is feeling anything.

The puzzle is this: you can't get something from nothing. If you start with ingredients that have zero experience, zero consciousness, zero inner life—and you just arrange them in different patterns—when does experience suddenly appear? At what level of complexity does the light turn on? And why?

The usual move is to say consciousness "emerges" from complex physical organization, the way liquidity emerges from H_2O molecules or the way traffic jams emerge from individual cars. But those analogies don't actually help. Liquidity is just a description of how molecules behave in aggregate—there's no mystery about how you get wetness from molecular motion. Traffic jams are just patterns we perceive—the cars don't suddenly become a new kind of entity.

Consciousness isn't like that. It's not just a description or a pattern. It's the undeniable felt reality of experience itself. And you can't derive felt experience from ingredients that have no capacity for feeling, no matter how cleverly you arrange them.

THE EXPLANATORY GAP

This brings us to the third problem, which is really a sharpened version of the second. Even if we describe in complete detail every physical process in your brain—every neuron firing, every chemical released, every electrical pattern—we still seem to have left out the most important thing: *what it feels like.*

Suppose neuroscience advances to the point where we can give a complete physical account of what happens in your brain when you see the color red. We can trace the light waves entering your eye, the signals transmitted to your visual cortex, the patterns of neural activation, and the cascade of chemical reactions. We can predict, with perfect accuracy, what you'll report seeing and how you'll behave. We have a complete physical story.

But have we explained why seeing red feels the way it does? Why there's a particular quality to that experience—the redness of red—that can't be captured in any amount of physical description?

You could know everything about the physics and chemistry of tasting chocolate without ever having tasted chocolate yourself. The experience itself seems to contain something more than, or different from, the physical processes that produce it. This is what philosophers call the explanatory gap: *the gap between physical description and felt experience.*

Now, maybe this gap will eventually be closed by better science. Maybe we'll discover how physical processes give rise to experience in a way that makes perfect sense, the way we now understand how temperature is really molecular motion. But it's also possible that the gap exists because our starting assumption is wrong—the assumption that the physical world is fundamentally unconscious stuff that somehow, mysteriously, produces consciousness.

WHAT THE PROBLEMS POINT TO

These three problems—observation affecting reality, consciousness emerging from non-consciousness, and the gap between physical description and felt experience—are not minor technical difficulties. They are signs that something is off in our basic picture.

Notice what they have in common: they all arise at the *boundary* between consciousness and the physical world. They all suggest that our usual way of thinking about this boundary might be the problem. We assume consciousness and matter are fundamentally different kinds of things—one mental, private, and subjective; the other physical, public, and objective—and then we tie ourselves in knots trying to explain how they connect.

What if the problem isn't that we haven't found the right connection? What if the problem is that we've started with a false separation?

The common-sense picture treats the world as made of unconscious stuff that exists entirely independently of experience, consciousness, or awareness. This stuff obeys mechanical laws and has no inner life. Consciousness, on this view, is either an illusion or a latecomer—something that mysteriously appears when you arrange the unconscious stuff in the right way.

But we've seen that this picture generates deep puzzles. It makes observation affecting reality inexplicable. It makes the emergence of consciousness mysterious. It opens an explanatory gap that seems unbridgeable.

These aren't just abstract philosophical problems. They are indications that we might be thinking about reality in a fundamentally flawed way—a way that creates problems that don't have solutions because the problems themselves are artifacts of our assumptions.

So what's the alternative? Before we can build a better picture, we need to look at the other obvious option: maybe it's not all unconscious stuff. Maybe it's all consciousness. Maybe the physical world is somehow mental, a construction or projection of the mind.

THE PROBLEM WITH PURE MIND

In the last chapter, we saw how treating the world as fundamentally made of unconscious stuff creates serious problems. When we try to explain consciousness, observation, and experience from a starting point of mindless matter, we end up with puzzles that seem unsolvable.

So here's a tempting thought: maybe we've got it backwards. Maybe the physical world isn't the foundation at all. Maybe consciousness is what's fundamental, and the material world is somehow derived from or dependent on the mind.

This isn't as crazy as it might first sound. After all, everything you know about the physical world comes to you through experience. You've never encountered a rock except through seeing it, touching it, or thinking about it. You've never measured an electron except through instruments that produce experiences—

pointer readings, screen displays, data you interpret. Every single thing you know about "the external world" is actually something you know through consciousness.

So why not take the bold step? Why not say that consciousness is all there is, and the physical world is a kind of organized experience—stable patterns in a fundamentally mental reality?

This view has a long and respectable history in philosophy. It's been defended by sophisticated thinkers for centuries. And it does solve some of the problems we identified in Chapter 1. If everything is fundamentally mental, then there's no mystery about how consciousness emerges—it doesn't emerge, it's there from the start. There's no explanatory gap between physical description and felt experience— experience is the fundamental reality, and physical descriptions are just useful ways of organizing our experiences.

But as we'll see, this view creates its own problems. And these problems are just as deep as the ones we were trying to escape.

THE STABILITY PROBLEM

If the physical world is just an organized experience or ideas in a mind, why is it so stable and consistent? Why does the table stay solid when you're not looking at it? Why does the sun rise tomorrow morning whether you're awake to experience it or not?

When you imagine a pink elephant, you can make it disappear at will. You can change its color, make it fly, or shrink it down to the size of a mouse. Your imagination is flexible, responsive to your wishes. But the real world isn't like that. You can't make the table disappear by willing it. You can't make gravity stop working because you'd prefer to float. The physical world has a stubborn independence that purely mental things don't seem to have.

The standard idealist response is to say that the physical world consists of ideas in a universal mind, not yours. But this just pushes the problem back. Why does the universal mind produce this particular stable world rather than some other world? If the answer is "because that's nature," we're essentially admitting that there's a structure or nature that constrains what happens—and that structure starts to look an awful lot like the physical laws we were trying to explain away.

More troubling still: if everything is mental, including the regularities we call physical laws, then what makes those laws binding? What stops them from changing? If it's "all in the mind," mental through and through, why do things behave as if there are objective, mind-independent constraints?

THE INTERSUBJECTIVITY PROBLEM

Here's a related but distinct puzzle. You and I seem to experience the same world. When we both look at the table, we see it in the same place, with the same shape, made of the same material. We can collaborate on building things, conducting experiments, and navigating spaces. The world presents itself consistently to different observers.

If the world is just my experience, just patterns in my consciousness, why do you experience it too? And why do our experiences match up so precisely?

The idealist might say: we all participate in the same universal mind, or our individual minds are somehow coordinated. But notice what's happening here. We're inventing elaborate structures to explain something that the common-sense view handles simply: there's a real world out there that we're all perceiving, and our perceptions match because they're perceptions of the same thing.

If you say the table is just an idea, but it's an idea we both have with perfect consistency, in exactly the same spatial relations to other ideas, responsive to our manipulations in exactly coordinated ways—well, at that point, what's the difference between your "idea of a table" and a real table? You've recreated the physical world in mental terms, but you haven't actually simplified anything. You've just changed the vocabulary.

THE PREDICTION PROBLEM

This brings us to perhaps the deepest problem with pure idealism. Science works. We can use mathematics to predict how things will behave with extraordinary precision. We can calculate when an eclipse will occur, how a bridge will bear weight, and what will happen when we collide particles at high energy. These predictions work because there are regular patterns in how things behave—patterns we can describe mathematically.

If the world is fundamentally mental, why is it mathematical? Why does nature seem to obey equations? Why can we use abstract formulas to predict concrete experiences?

You might say: because that's how the universal mind thinks. But this seems backwards. We discover mathematical patterns—we don't create them. The Pythagorean theorem is true whether anyone thinks about it or not. The orbit of Jupiter follows Kepler's laws, whether we've figured those laws out or not. There seems to be a structure to reality that exists independently of anyone's thinking about it.

If everything is mental, this independent structure is mysterious. Where does it come from? Why these patterns and not others? The physical realist has an answer: the patterns are in the nature of physical reality itself. The idealist has to invoke something—universal reason, pre-established harmony—that ends up looking suspiciously like objective reality smuggled back in through the back door.

THE PRACTICAL PROBLEM

There's also a more down-to-earth issue with saying

everything is mental. It doesn't help us do anything differently. When a doctor treats a patient, she needs to understand physiology, biochemistry, anatomy—all the details of how bodies actually work. Telling her "it's all really consciousness" doesn't change how she should proceed. The patterns she's studying—blood flow, chemical reactions, neural firing—behave according to their own regularities regardless of whether we call them physical or mental.

Similarly, when an engineer designs a bridge, he needs to calculate stress, tension, and weight distribution. The bridge will either stand or fall based on whether he gets the mathematics right. Knowing that the steel and concrete are "really" experiences or ideas doesn't change the calculations.

In other words, even if pure idealism is true, we still have to treat the world as if it has an objective, mind-independent structure. The supposed mental nature of reality makes no practical difference.

This isn't necessarily a fatal objection—maybe truth doesn't have to be practically useful. But it suggests that pure idealism isn't solving the problems we care about. It's just relabeling them.

WHAT WE'RE LEARNING

Let's step back and see what we've discovered in these first two chapters. We started with common sense: the world is made of unconscious stuff. This created deep problems about consciousness, observation, and experience. So, we considered the opposite: maybe everything is conscious, everything is mental. But this creates different deep problems about stability, intersubjectivity, and mathematical structure.

What's becoming clear is that neither extreme works. Reducing everything to unconscious matter doesn't work. Reducing everything to consciousness doesn't work either. The problems aren't solved by choosing sides—they're created by setting up sides in the first place.

Both views start by assuming that reality must be fundamentally one kind of thing: either stuff or experience, either objective or subjective, either matter or mind. Then, they try to derive or explain away everything else. But reality keeps refusing to cooperate with this agenda. The puzzles proliferate instead of dissolving.

Maybe that's the clue we need. Maybe the question isn't "Is it matter or mind?" Maybe that question itself embodies a false choice, based on assumptions we need to examine rather than accept.

What if reality isn't fundamentally made of things at all—whether those things are unconscious particles or conscious experiences? What if the basic character of reality is something else entirely, something that doesn't fit neatly into either category?

This is where we need to make a conceptual leap. Not a leap into mystery or vagueness, but a leap to a different kind of clarity—a way of thinking about reality that doesn't force us to choose between mind and matter because it starts from a different place entirely.

What If Nothing Stays Still?

We've seen that treating reality as fundamentally made of unconscious stuff creates problems, and treating it as fundamentally made of conscious experiences creates different problems. Both approaches start by assuming reality is made of things—either material things or mental things—and then try to explain everything else in terms of those basic building blocks.

But what if that assumption itself is the problem? What if reality isn't fundamentally made of things at all?

This sounds strange at first. Of course, the world is made of things. You're sitting on a chair, reading a book or looking at a screen. There are trees outside, cars on the street, and stars in the sky. Things are everywhere. How could reality not be made of things?

But let's look more carefully. What do we actually observe when we look at the world?

EVERYTHING CHANGES

Here's something you can verify right now, in your own experience: nothing stays exactly the same. Your body is constantly changing—cells dying, new ones forming, blood flowing, neurons firing. Your thoughts shift from moment to moment. The chair you're sitting on is aging, its molecules in constant motion. The "solid" table is mostly an empty space, with particles vibrating and quantum fields fluctuating.

Even things that seem permanent are changing. Mountains erode. Stars burn their fuel. Atoms decay. The universe itself is expanding, galaxies moving apart. At every scale, from the smallest to the largest, everything is in flux.

Now, our usual way of thinking about this is to say: things change. The chair exists, and it undergoes changes—it gets older, gets scratched, and eventually breaks. The mountain exists, and it undergoes erosion. We treat the thing as fundamental and change as something that happens to the thing.

But what if we've got this backwards? What if change is fundamental, and things are just stable patterns within the change?

Think about a flame. Is fire a *thing* that changes, or is it a *process*—a continuous transformation of fuel and oxygen into heat and light? You can't point to any particular molecule and say "that's the flame." The flame is the process itself, not any of the temporary participants in the process.

Or think about a river. Heraclitus, an ancient Greek philosopher, famously said you can't step in the same river twice. Why? Because the water is constantly flowing. The river isn't the water—it's the pattern of flow, the banks and bed and current that channel the water. The river is a process that persists through constant change.

Or think about yourself. The atoms that make up your body are constantly being replaced. You're not the same collection of particles you were seven years ago. Yet there's a continuity of pattern—your memories, your personality, your ongoing life. You are a process that maintains itself through constant transformation.

THE PROCESS VIEW

Here's the shift we need to make: instead of thinking of reality as made of things that change, think of it as made of processes—ongoing events, activities, happenings. Things are what we call *relatively stable patterns in these processes.*

This isn't just philosophical speculation. It's increasingly what science shows us. In quantum mechanics, what we call particles are better understood as excitations in quantum fields—ongoing vibrational patterns in something more fundamental. In biology, organisms are not static structures but self-maintaining processes, constantly exchanging matter and energy with their environment while preserving their organization. In neuroscience, the mind isn't a thing but an ongoing process of neural activity, constantly changing yet maintaining continuity.

Even something as apparently solid as a rock is, at the quantum level, a seething dance of particles and forces, held together in a stable pattern by constant interactions.

What seems solid and permanent is actually dynamic and temporary—but the patterns can be very long-lasting relative to our timescale, which is why we mistake them for permanent things.

WHY THIS MATTERS

This might seem like an abstract point, but it changes everything about our puzzles from the first two chapters.

Remember the measurement problem—the weird fact that observing something changes what it's doing? If we think of particles as tiny things with definite properties, this is baffling. But if we think of them as ongoing processes, patterns of activity in quantum fields, then interaction with another process (like a measuring device) naturally affects the pattern. The oddness evaporates.

Or remember the combination problem—how do you get consciousness from unconscious ingredients? If we're thinking of things—particles that either have consciousness or don't—this seems impossible. But if we're thinking of processes, with different degrees and kinds of activity, then the question changes. We're not asking how consciousness suddenly appears; we're asking how simple processes become complex, organized processes. That's still a deep question, but it's a tractable one.

The explanatory gap between physical description and felt experience also looks different. If we describe physical processes as movements of unconscious stuff, we've left out experience by definition. But if process itself has an interior character—if every activity is also an experience of some kind, however simple—then there's no gap to bridge. Physical description and experiential description are two ways of describing the same process, from outside and inside.

WHAT DOES A PROCESS LOOK LIKE?

Let's get concrete. What's an example of something that's clearly a process rather than a thing?

A conversation is a good example. A conversation isn't any of the individual words, or even the sum of the words. It's the back-and-forth, the flow of meaning, the mutual responsiveness of the participants. It exists only as it happens. You can't point to a conversation the way you can point to a rock. Yet conversations are real—they have effects, they can be profound or trivial, they create understanding or misunderstanding.

A melody is another example. The melody isn't any individual note. It's the pattern of notes over time, the relationships between them. Play the notes in a different order and you have a different melody. Speed them up or slow them down, and the melody changes character. The melody is pure process, pure pattern-in-time.

A thought is the same way. You can't freeze a thought and examine it as a static thing. Thoughts are events, happenings in your consciousness. They arise, develop, and pass away. Yet they're not nothing—they're real occurrences with real effects.

Now here's the radical proposal: what if everything is more like this than like a rock? What if even the rock is better understood as an ongoing process—a slow process, a stable process, but a process nonetheless?

STABILITY IN PROCESS

You might object: but things are stable! The table doesn't randomly dissolve. The laws of physics don't change. There is order and regularity in the world. How can you explain that if everything is just a process, just change?

This is a good question, but the answer is simpler than you might think. Processes can be stable. A spinning top, once set in motion, maintains its orientation through the very act of spinning. A bicycle stays upright because it's moving. An ecosystem maintains its character through constant change—species competing and cooperating, populations rising and falling, yet the overall pattern persists.

Stability doesn't require static things. In fact, stability often requires a constant process. Your body maintains its temperature through constant metabolic activity. Your identity persists through constant change. The patterns we call things are stable because they're active, not despite their activity.

The laws of physics, on this view, aren't rules that things obey. They are patterns in how processes unfold. They describe regularities in the way change happens. And these regularities emerge from the nature of the process itself, not from being imposed on the process from outside.

DIFFERENT KINDS OF PROCESS

Not all processes are the same. Some are simple and some are complex. Some are brief and some are long-lasting. Some are tightly organized, and some are chaotic.

A quantum event—a particle interaction, a photon emission—is a very simple process. It happens quickly and involves minimal organization.

A chemical reaction is more complex. Multiple atoms are involved, and their interactions follow specific patterns depending on their structure.

A living cell is vastly more complex still. It's a highly organized collection of processes—metabolic processes, regulatory processes, reproductive processes—all coordinated to maintain the cell's existence.

An organism is even more complex—multiple cells organized into tissues, organs, and systems, all working together.

An ecosystem is more complex yet—many organisms interacting, energy flowing through food webs, cycles of growth and decay, maintaining overall patterns.

And a conscious experience? That's one of the most highly organized processes we know of—billions of neurons firing in coordinated patterns, producing the unified experience of a moment of consciousness.

The point is: complexity and organization are matters of degree. There's no sharp line between "mere process" and "real thing." Everything is a process, but processes come in many forms, with many degrees of stability, complexity, and organization.

WHAT WE'VE GAINED

By shifting from things to processes, we've accomplished something important. We've found a way to think about reality that doesn't force us to choose between mind and matter.

Processes aren't purely mental or purely physical. A wave isn't in your mind, but it's not a solid object either. It's an activity, an event, something that happens. And this opens up new possibilities for thinking about consciousness and matter as different aspects or dimensions of the same fundamental reality—ongoing process.

We're not saying consciousness is an illusion or that matter is illusory. We're saying both are real features of processes. Physical description captures the external patterns, the regularities we can measure and predict. Experiential description captures the interior character, what it's like from the inside. Both are real, both are necessary for a complete picture, and neither is reducible to the other.

This might still seem abstract. We haven't yet explained exactly how this works or what it implies. But we've made a crucial move: we've shifted from asking "Is it matter or mind?" to asking "What kind of process is it, and what are its characteristics?"

That shift opens up everything that follows. Because once we stop thinking of consciousness and matter as two different kinds of stuff that somehow have to connect, we can start thinking of them as two aspects of process—and we can ask better questions about how process works, what its nature is, and why reality has the character it does.

EXPERIENCE GOES ALL THE WAY DOWN

In the last chapter, we shifted from thinking about reality as made of things to thinking about it as made of processes. This helped with some of our puzzles, but it raises a new question: what is the nature of these processes? What's actually going on in them?

We have two possible answers, and we've already seen the problems with both. We could say processes are purely physical—just matter in motion, energy transformations, particles interacting. But then we're back to the combination problem: how does consciousness emerge from purely unconscious process? We could say processes are purely mental—just experiences, ideas, consciousness, all the way. But then we're back to the stability problem: why do processes behave with such lawful regularity?

There is a third option, but it will sound strange at first. What if experience—in some form—is a basic

33

feature of process itself? Not just complex human consciousness, but something simpler and more fundamental. What if every process has both an outer aspect (what we can measure and describe physically) and an inner aspect (what it's like, however minimally, to be that process)?

This is the idea we need to explore carefully, because it is both the most counterintuitive and the most important part of our new picture of reality.

WHAT WE MEAN BY EXPERIENCE

First, let's be clear about what we're not saying. We're not claiming that electrons think, that atoms have opinions, or that rocks are pondering philosophy. That would be absurd, and it's not what we mean at all.

When we say experience might go all the way down, we need to distinguish between consciousness—the rich, complex, reflective awareness that humans have—and something more basic: simple responsiveness, minimal interiority, the barest hint of what it's like to be something.

Think about the difference between these things:

A thermostat responds to temperature. When it gets too cold, it turns the heat on. When it gets too warm, it turns the heat off. This is pure mechanical responsiveness—input triggers output. There's no reason to think the thermostat experiences anything. It's just a device following its design.

A bacterium also responds to its environment. It

moves toward nutrients and away from toxins. But unlike the thermostat, the bacterium is maintaining itself. It's not just responding mechanically—it's seeking, avoiding, preserving its own existence. Is there something it's like to be a bacterium? We can't know for certain, but the responsiveness is more integrated, more purposeful, more about the bacterium's own good.

A bee navigates using landmarks, communicates with other bees through dance, and remembers flower locations. The bee's behavior is flexible and adaptive in ways that suggest genuine learning and problem-solving. There's almost certainly something it's like to be a bee—some simple form of experience, awareness, sensation.

A human has all this and much more: self-awareness, abstract thought, language, and reflection on experience itself. We don't just experience—we know we experience. We can think about our thinking.

Now notice the pattern here. We don't have a sharp line where experience suddenly appears. We have a continuum: from minimal responsiveness to rich, reflective consciousness. The difference between bacteria and bees isn't that one has experience and the other doesn't—it's that the complexity and organization of experience differ dramatically.

THE PROPOSAL

Here's what we're suggesting: this continuum goes all

the way down. Not just to bacteria and bees, but to cells, to molecules, to atoms, to the most basic physical processes. Every process has some minimal interior character—something it's like, however simple, to be that process.

This doesn't mean a quark has thoughts or feelings like ours. It means that a quark's interaction with another quark has an interior aspect—a bare responsiveness, a minimal "taking account" of the other quark. Not conscious, taking account, not deliberate or reflective, but the most primitive form of responsiveness imaginable.

Why would we say this? What's the argument?

The argument is simple but powerful: if we start with processes that have zero interiority, zero experience, absolutely nothing it's like to be them, we can never explain how experience arises. You can't get something from nothing. Adding complexity doesn't help—lots of nothing is still nothing. A trillion unconscious processes don't somehow add up to one conscious experience.

But if we start with processes that have minimal interiority—the barest hint of experience—then we can explain how complex experiences arise. Complexity and organization transform a simple experience into a rich experience. Many simple processes, properly organized, become one unified complex process with correspondingly complex experience.

This is the difference between addition and

integration. Adding unconscious things never produces consciousness. But integrating experiential processes can produce new, more complex forms of experience.

HOW MUCH EXPERIENCE?

The crucial point is that experience comes in degrees—vast, almost unimaginable degrees of difference.

The "experience" of a fundamental particle—if we even want to call it that—is so minimal that it's barely worthy of the name. It's not sensation. It's not feeling. It's not anything we can imagine from our human perspective. It's just the bare fact that the particle's interaction with another particle has an interior character, however primitive.

A molecule has a slightly more complex "experience"—the integration of many atomic processes into one molecular process. Still nothing we'd recognize as sensation, but a tiny step up in complexity.

A cell has vastly more complex experience—millions of molecular processes coordinated to maintain the cell's life. Here we might begin to talk about something like primitive sensitivity, though still nothing like human feeling.

A simple animal has integrated millions of cells into a unified organism. Now we have something more clearly experiential—basic sensations, simple pleasures and pains, rudimentary awareness.

And a human integrates billions of neurons into the most complex process we know of, producing the rich, reflective consciousness we experience.

The differences between these levels are so enormous that it's almost misleading to use the same word—"experience"—for all of them. A quark's "experience" has as much in common with your reading this sentence as a single pixel has in common with a high-definition movie. The relationship is real, but the difference in complexity is almost infinite.

WHY THIS MATTERS

This view—that experience in some form is fundamental to process—solves several problems at once.

First, it solves the combination problem. We're not trying to get consciousness from non-consciousness. We're explaining how simple forms of experience, through organization and integration, become complex forms of experience. That's still a hard problem, but it's the kind of problem we know how to think about. Complexity and organization clearly matter for consciousness—brain damage can destroy aspects of experience, and brain development creates new capacities. If experience is fundamental, then complexity affects what kind of experience occurs, not whether experience occurs.

Second, it solves the explanatory gap. There's no gap between physical description and experience if every physical process has experiential character. Physical description tells us about the process from the outside—its structure, behavior, relationships. Experiential description tells us about the process from the inside—what it's like to be that process. Both descriptions are necessary and neither is reducible to the other, but they're describing the same reality from different perspectives.

Third, it helps with the measurement problem in quantum mechanics. If particles aren't just unconscious stuff but have minimal interiority, then interaction between particles isn't just mechanical collision—it's mutual influence between processes that each have their own character. The weirdness of quantum mechanics, where observation affects what's observed, becomes less weird if observation is always an interaction between experiential processes, not consciousness somehow magically affecting unconscious matter.

THE HARD PART

This view requires accepting something deeply counterintuitive: that what we think of as purely physical processes—particle interactions, chemical reactions, energy transformations—have an interior dimension we can't directly observe but must infer.

Why can't we observe it? Because we can only experience our own experience. I have direct access to what it's like to be me. I can infer that you have experience because you're similar to me—similar brain, similar behavior, similar reports. I can reasonably suspect my dog has experiences because she behaves in ways that suggest feeling and awareness. But I have no access whatsoever to what it's like to be a bacterium, let alone an atom.

The experiences of simple processes aren't just too faint for us to detect—they're *inaccessible in principle*. They're not experiences we could have or imagine. They're the interior character of processes that are nothing like our complex, organized consciousness.

So, we're making an *inference*: if complex, organized processes have rich experience (which we know from our own case), and if experience can't come from nothing, then simple processes must have simple experience. The alternative—that experience suddenly appears at some level of complexity—seems less plausible than accepting that experience is fundamental but varies enormously in form and complexity.

DEGREES, NOT KINDS

Here's another way to think about it. We're used to thinking about consciousness as something special, something that only certain complex organisms have. Either you have it or you don't. Either there's something it's like to be you, or there isn't.

But what if consciousness isn't a special addition to reality—what if it's a feature of reality in general, manifesting in wildly different forms depending on complexity and organization?

Think about life. At what point does something become alive? A virus? A self-replicating molecule? A protocell? There's no sharp boundary. Life is a matter of degree—certain processes (metabolism, reproduction, response to environment) that can be more or less present, more or less organized.

Or think about intelligence. Is a bee intelligent? A crow? A dolphin? A computer? Intelligence isn't all-or-nothing—it's a cluster of capacities (learning, problem-solving, adaptation) that come in many forms and degrees.

What we're suggesting is that experience is similar. It's not a yes-or-no property that magically appears at some point. It's a feature of the process itself, manifesting in countless different forms depending on the nature and complexity of the process.

Humans have extremely complex, organized, reflective experiences. Dogs have simpler but still rich experiences. Insects have a much simpler experience. Single cells have minimal experience. And even the simplest processes have the barest hint of interiority—not anything we'd recognize as sensation or feeling, but the primitive responsiveness that's the foundation for all more complex experience.

WHAT ABOUT COMPLEXITY?

You might ask: if even simple processes have

experience, why does complexity matter so much? Why are brain processes special?

The answer is integration. A rock contains trillions of atoms, each with its own minimal "experience." But these atomic processes aren't unified into one integrated process. They're not organized to work together toward anything. So, there is no unified experience of being a rock—just countless separate, unintegrated atomic processes.

A brain is different. The neurons are highly organized, constantly communicating, forming unified patterns of activity. Many processes become one process. Many simple experiences become one complex experience. That's what consciousness is: the integrated experience of a highly organized process.

This explains why brain damage can destroy specific aspects of consciousness. Disrupting the organization disrupts the integration. The individual neuronal processes continue, but they're no longer unified into the complex experience they were supporting.

It also explains why we can lose consciousness without dying. In deep sleep or under anesthesia, the neurons are still functioning, still processing. But they're not organized in the right way to produce an integrated, unified experience. The integration breaks down, and with it, consciousness as we know it disappears—though the underlying processes, with their own minimal experiential character, continue.

MAKING PEACE WITH THE STRANGE

We've now made the strangest claim in this book: that experience, in some minimal form, is fundamental to reality. That every process has an interior character. That the difference between a quark and a human isn't that one has experience and the other doesn't, but that human experience is incomparably more complex, organized, and unified.

This sounds bizarre. It violates our intuition that most of the universe is dead, unconscious matter, and that consciousness is rare and special.

But consider what we've gained. We've explained how consciousness fits into nature without being either miraculous (appearing from nothing) or illusory (not really existing). We've bridged the explanatory gap between physical processes and felt experience. We've made sense of how consciousness can be both real and natural, both irreducible and explicable.

And we've done this not by denying what science tells us about the physical world, but by recognizing that physical description is one way of describing reality—the exterior way—while experiential description is another way of describing the same reality—the interior way.

The physical world is real. The laws of nature are real. Chemistry and biology, and neuroscience are all studying real patterns in real processes. But those processes aren't dead, unconscious stuff mysteriously giving rise to consciousness. They're processes with their own minimal interior character, which becomes rich and complex when the processes themselves are richly and complexly organized.

This doesn't make electrons conscious in any sense we'd recognize. It makes consciousness natural in a way we can finally understand—not as a miraculous addition to an otherwise dead universe, but as a sophisticated development of something that was there all along in simpler form.

WHERE WE STAND

We've now taken the most challenging step in our journey. We've moved from thinking of consciousness as something rare and special to thinking of it as a complex form of something universal. Experience—in the broadest sense—is fundamental to process. What varies is the degree, the complexity, and the organization.

This might still feel uncomfortable. That's okay. Sit with it. The next chapter will help by showing how everything we've said fits together with another crucial insight: that processes don't exist in isolation. Everything is connected to everything else through relationships. And those relationships aren't external add-ons—they're constitutive of what things are.

Once we see how process and relationship work together, the picture becomes clearer and more compelling. We're building toward a view of reality where mind and matter, subject and object, consciousness and world are all aspects of one interconnected process—different ways of describing the same creative, evolving, participatory reality.

NOTHING EXISTS ALONE

We've established that reality is better understood as process than as things, and that processes have both exterior and interior aspects—what we can describe physically and what they're like from within. Now we need to add another crucial piece: processes don't exist in isolation. Everything is connected to everything else, and these connections aren't optional extras—they're essential to what things are.

This might sound obvious. Of course, things are connected. Your computer is connected to the internet. Your body is connected to the air you breathe. The Earth is connected to the Sun by gravity.

But we're making a stronger claim: things aren't just connected—they're constituted by their connections. What something *is* depends fundamentally on what it's related to.

Let's explore what this means and why it matters.

THE ILLUSION OF INDEPENDENCE

Think about an object you consider completely independent and self-contained—say, a coffee cup sitting on a table. It seems to exist entirely on its own, right? It has a definite shape, size, color, and weight. These properties seem to belong to the cup itself, regardless of anything else.

But look more carefully. The cup's color depends on the light hitting it—in red light, it looks red; in blue light, blue. Its weight depends on the gravitational field it's in—on the moon, it would weigh less. Its shape is stable only because of the electromagnetic forces holding its atoms together. Its very existence as a cup—as opposed to a meaningless clump of atoms—depends on human purposes and practices. Without beings who drink from vessels, it's just a shaped piece of ceramic.

Even at the most basic physical level, the cup's properties aren't self-contained. Each atom in the cup is in relationships with neighboring atoms—bonds that determine whether this is a solid ceramic or liquid clay. The electrons are in relationships with the nucleus— relationships we call electromagnetic force. The quarks that make up the protons are in relationships so tight they can't exist separately—trying to pull quarks apart just creates new quarks.

In other words, even this apparently independent object is actually a node in a vast network of relationships. And if we took away those relationships, we wouldn't have an independent cup—we wouldn't have anything at all.

RELATIONSHIP IN PHYSICS

Physics has been discovering the fundamental importance of relationships for over a century, though it's often expressed in technical language that hides the philosophical significance.

In quantum mechanics, particles don't have definite properties until they interact with something. An electron doesn't have a definite position—it exists in a blur of possibilities—until it interacts with a measuring device or another particle. Its properties are relational: they emerge from interaction, not from internal constitution alone.

This isn't just a weird feature of quantum mechanics. It's telling us something deep about the nature of reality. The idea that things first exist with definite properties and then interact is backwards. Interaction comes first. Properties emerge from a relationship.

In relativity, space and time aren't absolute containers in which things happen. They're aspects of relationships between events. Whether two events are simultaneous depends on your frame of reference. Whether a distance is long or short depends on how you're moving. Space and time are fundamentally relational.

The pattern is clear: the more deeply physics probes reality, the more it finds relationships rather than independent existence.

RELATIONSHIP IN BIOLOGY

Biology tells the same story even more clearly. No organism exists in isolation.

A tree seems like an independent thing, but it's actually embedded in countless relationships. Its roots are in a symbiotic relationship with fungi that help it absorb nutrients. It depends on bacteria in the soil that fix nitrogen. It depends on insects for pollination, birds for seed dispersal, the sun for energy, and the atmosphere for carbon dioxide. Remove these relationships and you don't have an independent tree— you have a dead tree.

More striking still: the tree's very identity is relational. What makes this collection of cells "a tree" rather than just cells? The organization—the way the cells are related to each other, differentiated into roots, trunk, branches, leaves, each playing a role in the life of the whole. The tree is a pattern of relationships, not a thing with relationships.

You can see this most clearly in your own body. You're not just a collection of cells. You're a highly organized system, where each part is defined by its relationships to the other parts. A heart cell is a heart cell because of where it is and what it does in relation to the rest of the body. Remove it from those relationships, and it's no longer really a heart cell—it's a dying cell in a petri dish.

And you're not even entirely "your" cells. Your gut contains trillions of bacteria—more bacterial cells than human cells. These bacteria are essential to your digestion, your immune system, and even your mood and behavior. Are they part of you or not? The question doesn't have a clear answer because the boundary isn't sharp. You're a biological process that includes relationships with countless other organisms.

RELATIONSHIP IN CONSCIOUSNESS

This relational character is even more obvious when we think about consciousness and thought.

Consider a concept—say, the concept of "tall." Tall means something only in relation to a context. A tall person isn't tall in absolute terms—they're tall compared to other people. A tall building is tall compared to other buildings. A tall ant would be short compared to a mouse. The concept has no meaning except in relation to a context of comparison.

Or consider your sense of self. Who you are depends profoundly on your relationships. You're someone's child, perhaps someone's parent, someone's friend, someone's colleague. Each relationship calls forth different aspects of who you are. You act differently with your parents than with your friends, differently with children than with peers. Which is the "real" you? All of them. Your identity is relational—it exists in and through your connections with others.

Even your perceptions are relational. When you see

the color of this page, that experience depends on the relationships between light, the page, your eyes, and your brain. Change any of these relationships, and the experience changes. Color isn't a property just of the object or just of your mind—it emerges from the relationship between them.

A thought never exists in isolation. Each thought arises in a context of other thoughts, memories, feelings, and perceptions. Its meaning depends on these relationships. The word "bank" means something different if you've just been thinking about rivers than if you've been thinking about money. The thought is shaped by its context—by what it's related to.

THE DEEPER PRINCIPLE

What all these examples point to is a fundamental principle: things are what they are because of their relationships, not in spite of them.

This flips our usual way of thinking. We tend to assume things first exist with their own independent nature, and then they enter into relationships with other things. A cup is made of ceramic, and then it sits on a table, and then light shines on it, and then you pick it up. The cup's nature is independent; the relationships are secondary.

But that's backwards. The "nature" of the cup—its solidity, its shape, its color, even its existence as a recognizable object—emerges from relationships. The electromagnetic bonds between atoms create solidity.

The interaction with light creates visible color. Your purposes and concepts make it a cup rather than just shaped matter.

This doesn't mean things are arbitrary or unreal. The cup is perfectly real. But its reality is relational reality. It exists as what it is because of how it's embedded in a web of relationships—physical, chemical, perceptual, and conceptual.

And this is true all the way down. An atom's properties emerge from the relationships of its parts. A quark's properties emerge from its relationships to other quarks and to quantum fields. There's no point where you reach something that exists independently, with its own nature unaffected by relationships. It's relationship all the way down.

INTERNAL AND EXTERNAL RELATIONS

Here's a useful distinction. Some relationships are external—they don't change what something is. If I move my cup from this table to that table, it's still the same cup. The relationship to the table doesn't constitute the cup's nature.

But other relationships are internal—they're essential to what something is. The relationship between a heart and a body is internal: a heart is essentially an organ-in-a-body. Remove that relationship, and you no longer have a heart in the meaningful sense.

The claim we're making is that many more

relationships are internal than we typically recognize. At the deepest levels, all relationships are internal. An electron is what it is because of its relationships to quantum fields, to other particles, to the structure of space-time. These aren't optional connections—they constitute what an electron is.

This means that to fully understand anything, you have to understand its relationships. You can't understand an organism without understanding its environment. You can't understand a word without understanding language. You can't understand a particle without understanding the fields it's embedded in.

Reality is fundamentally relational.

WHY THIS MATTERS

This relational understanding connects deeply with what we've already established about process and experience.

Remember, we said reality is better understood as process than as things. Now we're adding: processes are fundamentally relational. A process is an activity of connecting, relating, and integrating. It's not a thing relating to other things—it's relating itself, relationship as activity.

And remember, we said processes have interior character—some form of experience. Now we're adding: experience is essentially relational. To experience is to take account of something, to respond to something, to be affected by something. Experience is always experience-of. Even the simplest responsiveness of a fundamental particle is responsiveness-to another particle. The interiority and the relationality go together.

This is why it made sense to say that experience goes all the way down. If processes are fundamentally relational, and if relating involves taking account of what you're related to, then experience—understood as responsiveness, as being affected, as taking account—is inherent in the relational nature of process itself.

A particle "experiencing" another particle doesn't mean it's conscious of the other particle. It means the particle's process is shaped by, responsive to, and affected by the other particle's process. The relationship isn't just external collision—it's mutual influence, mutual participation in a shared process.

EVERYTHING IS CONNECTED

We can now make an even stronger claim: everything is connected to everything else, directly or indirectly.

The air you're breathing was once part of an ancient ocean, evaporated by the sun, carried by winds, fallen as rain, absorbed by plants, and released again. The atoms in your body were forged in stars billions of years ago, scattered across space when those stars exploded, and gathered into the cloud that formed our solar system. You're literally made of stardust, and those atoms will eventually return to the universe when your body breaks down.

But the connections aren't just historical. Right now, you're exchanging energy with your environment—radiating heat, absorbing light. You're gravitationally connected to every object in the universe, however minutely. The electromagnetic fields in your neurons are part of the universal electromagnetic field. The quantum fields that constitute your particles extend infinitely through space.

These connections are mostly negligible in practical terms. The gravitational influence of a distant star on your body is immeasurably tiny. But philosophically, they're significant. They show that nothing exists as a fully independent island. Everything is part of an interconnected whole.

This doesn't mean everything affects everything equally. Relationships have different strengths and different importance. Your relationship with the Earth's gravity is much more important for you than your relationship with a distant galaxy. Your relationship with your immediate environment matters more than your relationship with events on the other side of the planet.

But the principle stands: all processes are related, all are part of a larger whole, all are constituted in part by their connections to everything else.

PUTTING IT TOGETHER

Let's recap where we've gotten to:

Reality is fundamentally process—ongoing activity, change, happening. These processes have both exterior and interior aspects—what we can describe physically and what they're like from within. And these processes are fundamentally relational—what they are depends on what they're connected to.

This gives us a picture of reality that's profoundly different from the common-sense view we started with. Instead of independent things with properties, existing separately and then interacting, we have interconnected processes, each shaped by its relationships, each with both an outer structure and an inner character.

Consciousness fits naturally into this picture. It's not a mysterious addition to an otherwise dead universe. It's the interior aspect of highly organized, highly integrated processes. And it's necessarily relational—consciousness is always consciousness of something, experience is always experience shaped by relationships.

Matter fits naturally, too. It's not dead stuff that somehow gives rise to consciousness. It's the exterior aspect of processes, the patterns we can observe and measure and describe mathematically. Physical laws describe regularities in how processes relate to each other.

And the boundary between mind and matter, between inner and outer, between subject and object, starts to look different. These aren't separate realms that somehow have to connect. They're different aspects, different perspectives on the same relational processes.

But there's one more crucial piece we need to add. We've talked about how processes are relational, but we haven't yet explored the full implications of this for knowledge and understanding. If reality is fundamentally relational and participatory, then knowing isn't just passively receiving information about an independent reality. Knowing is itself a relationship—a way of participating in and shaping what is known.

You Help Make What You See

We've established three fundamental insights: reality is process, processes have interior character (experience), and processes are constituted by their relationships. Now we need to explore what might be the most personally significant implication of this view: knowing is not passive observation of an independent reality, but active participation in shaping what is known.

This sounds radical, maybe even absurd. Surely when you observe something—a tree, a star, a rock—you're discovering what's already there, not creating it. The tree existed before you looked at it. The star will exist after you stop looking. How can observation be participatory rather than passive?

Let's proceed carefully, because this is where misunderstanding is most likely. We're not claiming you can make things appear or disappear by wishing.

We're not saying reality is arbitrary or that you create the world through thought. We're making a more subtle but more profound claim: the act of knowing is itself a relationship, and like all relationships, it's mutual. What you know is shaped by how you know it, and what exists is shaped by how it's known.

THE QUANTUM CLUE

The clearest hint that observation isn't passive comes from quantum mechanics, which we touched on earlier. Let's look more carefully at what the experiments actually show.

In the famous double-slit experiment, you shoot electrons at a screen with two slits. If you don't observe which slit each particle goes through, they create an interference pattern—stripes of light and dark—as if each particle went through both slits and interfered with itself. But if you set up a detector to observe which slit each particle goes through, the interference pattern disappears. Now the particles behave as if each went through only one slit.

The act of observation changes the result. Not because the detector physically bumps the particle (careful experiments rule that out), but because observation itself affects what the particle is doing.

Here's what's crucial: before observation, the particle isn't secretly going through one slit or the other, while we just don't know which. It genuinely exists in a state where it's doing both. The observation doesn't reveal which slit it went through—it makes it go through one slit rather than both.

This isn't a measurement error or a temporary puzzle. It's a fundamental feature of quantum reality. The observer and the observed are not independent. The act of observing participates in determining what is observed.

Now, you might think this is just a weird feature of quantum mechanics that doesn't apply to everyday objects. And in practical terms, you'd be right. When you look at a tree, you're not making it be there. The tree is a large, stable process involving countless particles, and your observation doesn't significantly affect its overall behavior.

But philosophically, the quantum case shows us something important: the sharp separation between observer and observed, between consciousness and reality, isn't fundamental. At the deepest level, knowing and being are intertwined.

OBSERVATION AS INTERACTION

Let's think about what observation actually is. It's not magic vision rays shooting out of your eyes. It's a physical process: photons bounce off the tree, enter your eyes, trigger chemical reactions in your retina, send electrical signals to your brain, which processes them into the experience of seeing a tree.

Every step of this process involves interaction, relationship, and mutual influence. The photons affect your retina, and your retina (by absorbing the photons) affects the photon field. Your brain processes the signals, and this processing is shaped by your past experience, your expectations, and your focus of attention.

What you see isn't just "the tree as it is." It's the *tree-as-revealed-through-this-particular-way-of-interacting.* Change the interaction—use infrared cameras instead of visible light, use instruments instead of eyes, focus on different features—and you reveal different aspects of the tree.

Is there a tree apart from all possible ways of interacting with it? This is like asking if there's a melody apart from any possible performance. In one sense, yes—there's a score, a pattern. But the melody as actually experienced depends on the performance: the tempo, the instrument, the interpretation. The "tree itself" is the pattern of possible interactions, but any actual tree-as-experienced emerges from specific interactions.

This doesn't make the tree unreal or arbitrary. The tree constrains what interactions are possible. You can't interact with it as if it were water or air. But the tree-as-known is always the tree-as-revealed-through-interaction, never a pure "tree in itself" independent of any relationship.

ATTENTION SHAPES EXPERIENCE

You can verify this participatory character of knowing

in your own immediate experience, without any quantum mechanics.

Right now, you're reading these words. But you're also surrounded by other things: sounds, perhaps; the feeling of your body in the chair; the temperature of the air; countless visual details in your peripheral vision. All of this information is available, but most of it isn't in your awareness because you're not attending to it.

Now shift your attention. Notice a sound you weren't aware of before. Feel the weight of your body. Notice something in your peripheral vision. The moment you attend to these things, they come into focus. They were there before, but they weren't part of your experienced reality until you attended to them.

Attention doesn't create things from nothing. But it does shape what appears in your experienced world. Two people in the same room can have quite different experiences depending on what they attend to. A musician hears subtleties in music that others miss. A botanist sees distinctions between plants that others don't notice. An expert chess player sees patterns on the board that a novice doesn't perceive.

These aren't just different interpretations of the same experience. They're different experiences. What appears in consciousness depends on how consciousness engages with the world. The engagement is *participatory*—you're not passively receiving a pre-formed reality, you're actively participating in bringing aspects of reality into experiential focus.

Here's another everyday example of participation. The questions you ask determine what answers you can find.

If you ask "What color is the tree?" you'll discover one set of facts about the tree. If you ask "How old is the tree?" you'll discover different facts. If you ask "What species is the tree?" you'll discover yet other facts. Each question reveals something real about the tree, but which aspect of reality gets revealed depends on the question asked.

This is obvious in conversation. Ask someone, "How are you feeling?" and you'll get information about their emotional state. Ask "What have you been working on?" and you'll get information about their activities. Same person, different questions, different aspects revealed.

But it's true more generally. Science progresses by asking better questions, not just by making better observations. Newton asked, "What force makes things move?" and discovered the laws of motion. Einstein asked, "What if the speed of light is constant?" and discovered relativity. The questions didn't create gravity or relativity, but they did determine which aspects of reality became visible.

Questions are ways of engaging with reality, and different engagements reveal different features. Reality responds to how you approach it. This is participation: your mode of engagement matters for what gets revealed.

LEVELS OF PARTICIPATION

We can now distinguish different levels or kinds of participation in knowing.

At the quantum level, observation directly affects what state the system is in. This is strong participation—the act of measuring participates in determining the result.

At the biological level, organisms actively explore their environment, selecting and interpreting information based on their needs and capacities. A bee sees ultraviolet patterns on flowers that humans don't see. A bat experiences the world through echolocation in ways we can barely imagine. Each organism participates in constructing its own experienced world from the available information.

At the human level, we have multiple forms of participation. Attention selects what appears in consciousness. Concepts shape how we categorize and understand what we experience. Expectations influence what we perceive—you're more likely to see what you expect to see. Language carves up experience in particular ways—different languages make different distinctions available.

And at the social level, we collectively construct shared realities. Money has value because we collectively agree it does. Laws exist because we collectively recognize them. Scientific facts are established through community practices of observation, experimentation, and verification. These aren't arbitrary inventions, but they are participatory constructions—they exist through our collective engagement with reality.

NOT SUBJECTIVISM

We need to be very clear about what we're not saying. We're not saying reality is whatever you think it is. We're not saying you can change the world by changing your mind. We're not endorsing wishful thinking or "manifest your reality" nonsense.

Reality pushes back. You can't walk through walls by believing you can. You can't make the sun rise at midnight by wanting it to. The world has structure, patterns, and regularities that exist independently of what any individual thinks or wants.

What we're saying is more subtle: the patterns and regularities of reality are revealed through interaction, and different modes of interaction reveal different patterns. The world isn't formless—it has structure. But which aspects of that structure become manifest depends on how you engage with it.

Think of it this way: a sculpture contains many possible views—front, back, side, from above, from below. Each view is real, showing genuine features of the sculpture. But which view you see depends on where you stand. You don't create the sculpture by looking at it, but what you see is shaped by your relationship to it. And the "complete" sculpture is the unity of all possible views, never fully captured in any single perspective.

Reality is like this, but more so. It's not that there's a fixed reality and we just see different perspectives on it. It's that reality is fundamentally responsive—it actualizes different potentials depending on how it's engaged. The electron isn't secretly going through one slit—it genuinely has the potential for both, and observation actualizes one potential rather than another.

PARTICIPATORY KNOWLEDGE

This gives us a new understanding of what knowledge is. Knowledge isn't a mirror reflecting an independent reality. It's not a representation that's accurate or inaccurate, true or false, in a simple correspondence with external facts.

Knowledge is a mode of participation in reality. It's a relationship between knower and known where both are affected, where what is known depends partly on how it's known, where the activity of knowing is itself part of the reality being known.

This doesn't make knowledge arbitrary or unreliable. Good knowledge is knowledge that establishes effective, stable, productive relationships with reality. Science works because it finds reliable modes of interaction that reveal consistent patterns. But these patterns aren't simply "out there" waiting to be discovered—they emerge in the interaction between our modes of inquiry and the responsive structure of reality.

Different modes of inquiry reveal different aspects. Physics reveals mathematical patterns. Biology reveals functional organization. Psychology reveals experiential structure. None of these is the "one true" description of reality. Each is a valid mode of participation that reveals genuine features.

And because reality is fundamentally process, fundamentally relational, this makes sense. To know a process is to participate in it, to relate to it, to let it affect you and to affect it in turn. Complete, perfect, detached knowledge—the view from nowhere—is impossible not because we're limited, but because knowing is inherently relational and therefore inherently participatory.

THE CIRCLE CLOSES

Now we can see how everything fits together:

Reality is process—an ongoing, creative activity. Processes have interior and exterior aspects— experience and physical structure. Processes are fundamentally relational—constituted by their connections. And knowing is itself a process, a relationship, a mode of participation.

Consciousness isn't separate from reality, observing

it from outside. Consciousness is reality becoming aware of itself, processes complex enough to know other processes and to know themselves. You are not an isolated mind looking out at an external world. You are a process embedded in and emerging from the larger process of reality, in constant participatory relationship with everything around you.

This dissolves the puzzles we started with. The measurement problem in quantum mechanics isn't weird—it's showing us the participatory character of reality. Observation affects what's observed because observation is participation. The combination problem dissolves—consciousness doesn't emerge from unconscious matter; it develops as processes become more complex and integrated. The explanatory gap closes—there's no gap between physical process and experience because they're interior and exterior aspects of the same participatory reality.

WHAT THIS MEANS

Understanding knowing as participation changes how we relate to reality.

If knowledge is passive observation, you're fundamentally separate from what you know. The world is "out there," you're "in here," and knowledge is a bridge between separate realms. This creates a sense of alienation—you're fundamentally cut off from reality, only able to observe it from outside.

But if knowledge is participation, you're not

separate from reality—you're part of it, engaged with it, responsive to it and helping to actualize it. This doesn't mean you control reality or that reality depends on you. It means you're in a genuine relationship with reality, not isolated from it.

This has practical implications. In science, it means recognizing that observation isn't neutral—how we set up experiments matters for what we discover. In personal life, it means recognizing that how we attend to things shapes what we experience. In social life, it means recognizing that we collectively participate in creating shared realities—institutions, meanings, values—that are real but not fixed.

Most fundamentally, it means recognizing that you're not just an observer of reality but a participant in it. Your consciousness, your choices, your actions, your attention—all of these are ways of participating in the ongoing creative process of reality.

This is empowering and humbling at once. Empowering because your participation matters— you're not just watching reality unfold, you're part of how it unfolds. Humbling because you're one participant among countless others, and reality is vastly larger than your individual perspective.

PULLING BACK

We've now covered the core ideas: process, experience, relation, and participation. These four concepts work together to give us a picture of reality that's very different from the common-sense view we started with, but that solves the puzzles that view created.

In the next chapter, we'll step back and see how all these pieces fit into a coherent whole. We'll see how this view—let's call it participatory process reality—gives us a way to understand consciousness and matter, mind and body, subject and object, as different aspects of one unified reality. We'll see what we've gained and what questions remain.

And then, in the final chapter, we'll explore what this means for how we understand ourselves and live our lives. Because philosophy isn't just about abstract ideas—it's about understanding our place in reality and how to inhabit that place well.

But first, let's put the pieces together.

Putting It Together

We've covered a lot of ground in the last chapters. Let's pause and see how it all fits together into one coherent picture.

We started with a problem: the common-sense view that reality is made of unconscious stuff creates deep puzzles about consciousness, observation, and experience. The alternative—saying everything is mental—creates different but equally serious puzzles about stability, intersubjectivity, and why the world behaves lawfully.

Then we made four crucial moves:

First, we shifted from things to processes. Reality isn't fundamentally made of static objects that change; it's made of ongoing activities, events, happenings. Things are stable patterns in process, not fundamental building blocks.

Second, we recognized that processes have an interior character—some form of experience, however minimal. Not human-like consciousness all the way down, but responsiveness, sensitivity, taking-account-of. Experience varies enormously in complexity, but it's present in some form at every level.

Third, we saw that processes are fundamentally relational. Nothing exists in isolation. What something is depends on what it's connected to. Relationships aren't optional extras—they constitute the nature of things.

Fourth, we understood that knowing is participatory. You don't passively observe an independent reality from outside. You actively participate in reality through the relationships you establish with it. What you know depends partly on how you know it.

Now we need to see how these four insights work together to give us a unified picture—a way of understanding reality that doesn't force us to choose between mind and matter, between consciousness and the physical world.

THE BASIC PICTURE

Here's the core idea: reality is an ongoing creative process, fundamentally relational and experiential, manifesting in countless forms at different scales of complexity and organization.

Let's unpack that carefully.

"Ongoing creative process" means reality isn't static. There's no final, complete state that everything is heading toward or resting in. Reality is constantly becoming, constantly actualizing new possibilities. The future isn't predetermined—it emerges from the interaction of present processes.

"Fundamentally relational" means processes don't exist independently and then interact. The interactions, the relationships, are what processes are. To be is to be related, to be connected, to be affecting and being affected.

"Experiential" means every process has an interior aspect—what it's like, however minimally, to be that process. This isn't consciousness in the human sense for most processes. It is responsiveness, taking-account-of, being affected by relationships.

"Manifesting in countless forms" means this basic character—process, relational, experiential—shows up differently at different scales. A quantum interaction is very simple. A chemical reaction is more complex. A living cell is vastly more complex. A conscious organism is more complex still. But they're all variations on the same theme: process, relation, experience.

HOW MIND FITS IN

On this view, mind—consciousness, experience, awareness—isn't a special substance added to an otherwise mindless universe. It's a sophisticated development of something that was there all along in simpler form.

The simplest processes have the barest hint of experiential character—minimal responsiveness to other processes. As processes become more complex and organized, their experiential character becomes richer. Many simple processes, properly organized and integrated, become one complex process with correspondingly complex experience.

Your consciousness right now—reading these words, thinking about these ideas, perhaps feeling curious or skeptical or tired—is the integrated experience of billions of neuronal processes working together. Each neuron is itself a complex process with its own minimal experiential character. But they're organized into larger patterns—neural assemblies, brain regions, whole-brain states—and these larger patterns have their own unified experiential character. That's what consciousness is: a highly organized, highly integrated process experiencing itself.

This explains several puzzling features of consciousness. It explains why brain organization matters so much—damage the organization and you damage the unified experience. It explains why consciousness seems to come in degrees—from deep sleep to drowsy to alert to intensely focused—because the degree of integration varies. It explains why different brain regions support different aspects of experience—vision, memory, emotion—because different patterns of organization produce different forms of experience.

And it explains why consciousness seems both physical and non-physical, both part of nature and somehow transcendent. Physical description captures the exterior aspect of the process—the neural firing patterns, the information flow, the measurable structures. Experiential description captures the interior aspect—what it feels like, what it's like to be that process. Both are real. Both are necessary. Neither is reducible to the other.

HOW MATTER FITS IN

Matter, on this view, isn't dead stuff. It's the exterior aspect of process—what process looks like from the outside, what we can measure and describe mathematically.

When we do physics, we're studying patterns in how processes relate to each other. Mass, charge, momentum, energy—these are all ways of describing relational properties of processes. They're perfectly real, perfectly objective in the sense that they're stable patterns that everyone can discover. But they're not properties of independently existing things—they're patterns in an ongoing process.

This is why physics is so successful with mathematics. Mathematics is the language of pattern and relationship. If reality is fundamentally processual and relational, then mathematical description naturally captures its structure. The universe isn't somehow "made of math," but mathematical patterns are inherent in how processes relate.

It also explains why physics keeps discovering the importance of relationships. Quantum entanglement shows particles in an ongoing relationship even across distances. Relativity shows space and time are relational rather than absolute. Field theories show particles as excitations in fields—patterns in something more fundamental. All these discoveries point to relationality and process as basic.

And it explains why observation affects what's observed at the quantum level. If observation is itself a process relating to other processes, and if processes are shaped by their relationships, then observation naturally affects what happens. There's no spooky action, no consciousness mysteriously influencing matter. There's just process relating to process, as always happens.

How They Connect

The deepest insight is this: mind and matter aren't two different substances or realms that somehow have to connect. They're two aspects of one reality—process.

Think of it this way. A coin has two sides—heads and tails. Neither side is more real or more fundamental. You can't have heads without tails or tails without heads. They're two aspects of one thing.

Or think of a wave. You can describe it from the outside—wavelength, amplitude, frequency. Or you can experience it from within—riding the wave, feeling its rise and fall. The descriptions are different, but they're describing the same wave, from different perspectives.

Reality is like this, but more fundamentally. Every process has an exterior aspect (its structure, its relationships, its measurable properties) and an interior aspect (its experiential character, what it's like to be that process). These aren't two separate things stuck together. They are two ways of engaging with the same reality.

This means there's no interaction problem—no mystery about how the mind affects the body or body affects mind. Your decision to lift your arm and your arm lifting aren't two separate events that mysteriously coordinate. They're one event—a process that has both experiential character (your intention, your sense of effort) and physical structure (neural signals, muscle contractions). Described from the inside, it's willing. Described from the outside, it's neural activity. Both descriptions are valid. Both capture real features. Neither is complete without the other.

WHAT WE'VE GAINED

Let's be clear about what this view accomplishes.

It solves the measurement problem in quantum mechanics. Observation isn't weird—it's just a process relating to process, and processes naturally affect each other through relationships.

It solves the combination problem. We're not trying

to get consciousness from non-consciousness. We're explaining how simple experiential processes, through organization and integration, become complex experiential processes.

It closes the explanatory gap. There's no gap between physical description and felt experience because they're interior and exterior descriptions of the same processes.

It makes consciousness natural. Consciousness isn't a miracle or an illusion. It's a sophisticated development of experiential process—rare in the universe because the right kind of organization is rare, but not fundamentally alien to the nature of reality.

It makes science and experience both valid. Science studies the exterior patterns of processes. Direct experience reveals their interior character. Neither is more real or more fundamental. We need both for a complete understanding.

And it makes us participants in reality rather than external observers. We're not isolated minds locked in bodies, observing an alien external world. We're processes embedded in the larger process of reality, in constant participatory relationship with everything around us.

WHAT REMAINS MYSTERIOUS

This view doesn't answer everything. Deep mysteries remain, but they're different mysteries from the ones we started with.

Why is there something rather than nothing? Why does process take the forms it does? Why these laws of nature rather than others? These questions remain. But at least we're asking them about one coherent reality, not about two fundamentally different realms that mysteriously connect.

Why does complexity lead to consciousness specifically? We've explained that complex, organized processes have complex experience, but we haven't explained in detail how neural organization produces the specific qualities of human consciousness—colors, sounds, emotions, thoughts. That remains a deep question, though it's now a tractable scientific question rather than a philosophical puzzle.

How does the brain create a unified experience from billions of separate neural processes? We know it does—we experience unity despite neural complexity. But the mechanisms of integration are still being discovered. This is an active area of neuroscience research.

And the biggest question: what is the ultimate nature of process itself? We've said reality is process, but what is process? What makes it be rather than not be? What drives the ongoing creativity of reality? These might be unanswerable questions—limits of what can be known from within reality. Or they might have answers we haven't yet discovered.

THE DIFFERENCE IT MAKES

You might ask: Does this view make any practical difference? If it doesn't change how we do science or live our lives, why does it matter?

It matters because how we understand reality shapes how we experience it and how we act in it.

If you think consciousness is a fluke, an accident, an anomaly in an otherwise dead universe, you experience yourself as fundamentally alien to reality. You're a ghost in a machine, an awareness trapped in unconscious matter, forever separate from the world you observe.

But if you understand consciousness as natural, as a sophisticated development of something fundamental to reality itself, you experience yourself differently. You're not alien to reality—you're part of it. Your awareness, your experience, your choices—these aren't anomalies. They're reality becoming conscious of itself, participating in its own ongoing creativity.

This changes how you relate to nature. Instead of seeing the natural world as dead resources to be exploited, you recognize it as process, as activity, as having its own forms of interiority, however different from yours. This doesn't mean you can't use nature— you're part of nature and your use is natural too. But it changes the quality of the relationship.

It changes how you think about other people. Instead of seeing them as separate minds behind barriers of skin and skull, you recognize that consciousness is fundamentally relational, that your awareness and theirs exist in ongoing mutual influence, that understanding them isn't just guessing at hidden mental states but participating in shared experiential processes.

It changes how you think about knowledge. Instead of trying to observe reality from outside with perfect detachment, you recognize that knowing is participating, that your engagement matters, that different questions reveal different aspects of reality. This makes knowledge more humble (you're always limited by your particular mode of engagement) and more empowering (your engagement actually matters).

And it changes how you think about your place in the universe. You're not an isolated observer watching reality unfold. You're a participant in an ongoing creative process. Your choices, your attention, your relationships—all of these are ways the universe becomes conscious of itself and shapes its own future. You matter, but not because you're separate from reality. You matter because you're part of it.

THE JOURNEY SO FAR

We started with puzzles: how consciousness relates to matter, how observation affects what's observed, how experience arises from unconscious ingredients. We saw that the common-sense view—reality as unconscious stuff—creates these puzzles. And we saw that the opposite view—reality as pure consciousness—

creates different but equally serious puzzles.

Then we found a way beyond the either-or: reality as process, relational and experiential, manifesting in countless forms. Mind and matter aren't separate realms but aspects of one processual reality. Consciousness isn't miraculous or illusory but natural—a sophisticated development of experiential process.

This gives us a coherent picture, one that includes both the regularities science discovers and the experiences we live through. It makes consciousness part of nature without reducing it to mere brain states. It makes matter real without making it dead. It makes knowing participatory without making it arbitrary.

We have one more step. In the final chapter, we'll explore what this means for living—for how we understand ourselves, how we relate to others, how we inhabit our place in reality. Because philosophy isn't just about understanding—it's about living well in light of that understanding.

WHAT THIS MEANS

We've now built a complete picture: reality is an ongoing creative process, fundamentally relational and experiential, manifesting as both mind and matter depending on how we engage with it. But understanding is only valuable if it shapes how we live. So what does this view mean for how we understand ourselves and our place in reality?

Let's explore the implications, moving from how we understand consciousness to how we understand ourselves, our relationships, and our participation in the ongoing creativity of reality.

UNDERSTANDING CONSCIOUSNESS

On the view we've developed, consciousness isn't a puzzle to be solved—it's a pointer to something fundamental about reality.

The fact that you're conscious, that there's

something it's like to be you, that you have experiences and awareness—this isn't an anomaly requiring special explanation. It's reality doing what reality does: process experiencing itself. You're not an unlikely accident in an otherwise unconscious universe. You're reality becoming conscious of itself in a particular, highly organized way.

This changes the question from "How does consciousness arise from unconscious matter?" to "How does simple experiential process become complex experiential process?" That's still a deep question, but it's a natural question. It's asking about organization and complexity.

It also means consciousness isn't fundamentally private and isolated. Your experience is your experience, unique to you, but it's not sealed off from reality. Consciousness is inherently relational—it's always consciousness of something, shaped by relationships, existing through participation. You're not trapped inside your own mind, cut off from everything else. You're embedded in reality, in constant relationship with it.

This has a practical implication: you can trust experience. Not uncritically—experience can be mistaken, partial, distorted. But experience is a genuine way of engaging with reality, not a distorting screen between you and the world. When you see a tree, you're not seeing a representation of a tree—you're in direct relationship with the tree through vision. The experience is real contact with a real process.

If experience is real engagement with reality, what about science? Science deliberately excludes subjective experience, focusing on what can be measured and replicated. Does that make it a distortion?

No. Science is a particular mode of engagement— one that focuses on the exterior, measurable, predictable aspects of process. This is enormously valuable. By systematically studying patterns from the outside, science discovers regularities that hold across different observers, different contexts, and different times. These regularities are real. They're stable features of how processes relate to each other.

But scientific description is incomplete. It captures the exterior of processes but not their interior. It tells us how things behave but not what they experience. A complete neuroscience could describe every physical process in your brain when you see red, but it would still leave out the redness—the felt quality of the experience.

This doesn't mean science is wrong or that we need something else instead of science. It means we need science plus acknowledgment of the interior aspect that science necessarily excludes from its methods. Physical description and experiential description are both necessary. Neither is complete without the other.

In practice, this means respecting both scientific

investigation and direct experience. Science discovers patterns in the exterior aspects of reality. Experience reveals the interior aspects. Good understanding integrates both—using science to understand structures and regularities, using experience to understand what those structures and regularities feel like from within.

UNDERSTANDING AGENCY

One of the persistent worries about seeing ourselves as part of nature is that it seems to eliminate genuine agency. If you're just a physical process following natural laws, how can you be truly free? How can your choices matter?

But on the view we've developed, this worry dissolves. You're not just a physical process—you're a process with both exterior and interior aspects. The exterior aspect follows physical regularities. But the interior aspect—your experience, your deliberation, your choice—is equally real. It's not a separate magical force intervening in the physical world. It's the interior of the same process that physics describes from the outside.

When you make a choice, something real happens. Possibilities are evaluated, options are weighed, and a decision emerges. This process has physical correlates—neural activity, brain states. But it also has experiential reality—what it feels like to deliberate, to decide, to commit. Both descriptions capture real features of the same process.

Your agency isn't freedom from natural process. It's a particular form of natural process—complex, organized, reflective process that integrates information, evaluates possibilities, and determines action. The fact that this process is natural doesn't make it less real or less yours.

In fact, recognizing that you're a natural process embedded in larger processes makes agency more intelligible, not less. Your choices emerge from the interaction of your past experience, your current situation, your goals and values. They're not random—they're expressions of who you are, which is itself a pattern of organized process. That's not determinism in the sense that makes agency illusory. That's what real agency is: action that emerges from your own organized complexity.

UNDERSTANDING VALUE

If consciousness is natural, if we're part of an ongoing process rather than separate observers, what about value? Does anything really matter, or is everything just a neutral process?

Value, on this view, is also natural. Value emerges from the experiential character of process itself.

Consider: some experiences feel good and some feel bad. Pleasure and pain, satisfaction and frustration, joy and suffering—these aren't arbitrary labels we apply to neutral processes. They're intrinsic features of experience itself. Experience has valence—a positive or negative quality—built into it.

This means value is real. Suffering really is bad—not because some authority declares it bad, but because of what suffering is, what it feels like. Joy really is good—not because we've decided to value it, but because of its intrinsic character.

And because experience goes all the way down (in varying forms and degrees), value goes all the way down too. A plant's response to sunlight, an animal's satisfaction of hunger, a person's achievement of understanding—these all involve simple or complex forms of positive value. The flourishing of any process has value intrinsic to that process.

This doesn't mean all values are equal or that we should treat all processes the same. More complex, more integrated, more conscious processes have richer value. The suffering of a human matters more than the "suffering" (if we even call it that) of a bacterium because human experience is vastly more complex and unified. But the principle is the same: value emerges from experiential process.

For living, this means recognizing that value is real and natural. Ethical choices matter because they affect experiential processes—your own and others'. The goal is to participate well in the ongoing process of reality, promoting flourishing and reducing suffering wherever you can effectively do so.

UNDERSTANDING OTHERS

If consciousness is fundamentally relational and participatory, what does this mean for how we understand other people?

First, it means other minds aren't fundamentally inaccessible mysteries. We tend to think we're locked inside our own consciousness, only able to guess at what others experience. But consciousness isn't locked inside anything. It exists through relationship, through participation in shared processes.

When you have a conversation with someone, you're not exchanging signals that allow you to infer their hidden mental states. You're participating in a shared process—a conversation is itself an experiential process that both of you are part of. Understanding someone isn't mainly guessing—it's participating well in the shared process of communication.

This is why empathy is possible. You can understand how someone feels not mainly by logical inference but by entering into a relationship with them, letting their experiential process affect yours. This isn't magic—it's the natural responsiveness of experiential processes to each other.

It also means that relationships are fundamental to who you are, not optional additions. You're not a self-contained individual who then chooses to relate to others. You're constituted by your relationships. Who you are emerges from your connections—with family, friends, community, culture. These aren't external to your identity—they're essential to it.

Practically, this suggests taking relationships seriously as fundamental realities, not just as instrumental means to individual ends. The relationships themselves matter, not just what they provide to isolated individuals. Caring for relationships is caring for something real and valuable, not just maintaining useful connections.

UNDERSTANDING OUR PLACE

Pulling back to the largest scale: what's our place in reality?

On the view we've developed, we're not aliens in an indifferent universe. We're not cosmic accidents or improbable flukes. We're not ghosts haunting machines or consciousness trapped in dead matter.

We're reality becoming conscious of itself. We're complex organized processes that have developed the capacity for reflection, for understanding, for choice. We're participants in the ongoing creative advance of reality, not external observers watching it unfold.

This is simultaneously humbling and empowering. Humbling because we're not central or special in an absolute sense—consciousness appears in many forms, at many levels, and human consciousness is just one relatively recent development.

But empowering because we do genuinely matter. Our consciousness, our choices, our actions—these are ways reality shapes itself. We're not just watching—

we're participating. What we do has real effects on how the process unfolds.

This suggests an attitude toward life that's neither nihilistic nor grandiose. Not nihilistic because value is real, choices matter, and consciousness is a genuine expression of reality's nature. Not grandiose because we're one form of consciousness among many, embedded in processes vastly larger than ourselves, dependent on relationships we don't control.

The right attitude is something like humble participation. We're part of something larger than ourselves, and we can participate well or poorly. Participating well means: being conscious, being present, being attentive to experience. It means understanding as deeply as we can, choosing as wisely as we can, relating as genuinely as we can.

LIVING IN PROCESS

Finally, what does it mean to live consciously in light of this understanding?

It means recognizing that you're not a static thing but an ongoing process. Your identity isn't fixed—it's constantly being created through your choices, your relationships, your engagement with reality. You're always becoming, always actualizing new possibilities.

This makes change less threatening and growth more natural. You don't have a fixed nature that change disturbs. You're inherently changing, inherently creative, inherently responsive to new experiences and relationships.

It means recognizing that the present moment is where reality actually happens. The past is gone—it exists now only as influence, as pattern, as memory. The future hasn't happened—it exists now only as possibility, as potential, as direction. Reality is always now, always this moment of process actualizing itself. Being fully present isn't just a technique—it's aligning with the fundamental nature of reality as an ongoing process.

It means recognizing that relationships are where your life actually happens. You're not preparing for life through your relationships—your relationships are your life. The connections you form, the way you engage with others, the mutual influence and shared experience—this is where you exist most fully.

It means trusting both thinking and feeling as forms of engagement with reality. Thinking reveals patterns, structures, and regularities. Feeling reveals value, meaning, and significance. Both are real ways of knowing, and both capture genuine aspects of process. Good living integrates both—using thought to understand structure, using feeling to respond to value.

And it means accepting your finitude while recognizing your significance. You won't live forever. Your consciousness is temporary, dependent on a delicate organization that will eventually fail. But while you're here, you're genuinely participating in reality. You're one way reality becomes conscious of itself.

Your experience is real. Your choices matter.

THE INVITATION

This book has offered you a way of understanding reality: as an ongoing creative process, fundamentally relational and experiential, manifesting as both mind and matter depending on how we engage with it.

This isn't just an abstract theory. It's an invitation to experience reality differently—not as an external object you observe, but as an ongoing process you participate in. Not as dead matter you manipulate, but as a responsive process you relate to. Not as a puzzle to solve from outside, but as a reality to inhabit more fully.

Philosophy, at its best, isn't just about getting the theory right. It's about living differently in light of understanding. If this view makes sense to you, then the question is: how does it change how you engage with your own consciousness, with other people, with the natural world, with the ongoing creative process of reality itself?

That's not a question this book can answer for you. It's a question you answer through living—through the choices you make, the attention you bring, the relationships you form, the way you participate in the ongoing creativity of reality.

We started with puzzles about consciousness and matter. We end with an understanding that makes those puzzles dissolve—not by finding clever answers, but by recognizing that the questions were based on false assumptions about separation between mind and world.

Consciousness and matter are not two fundamentally different things mysteriously connected. They're two aspects of one reality—process, creative, relational, experiential, ongoing. You are not an isolated observer of this reality. You are an expression of it, a participant in it, a way it becomes conscious of itself.

That's not everything we might want to know. Deep mysteries remain. But it's enough to live by. It's enough to make sense of experience, to trust consciousness, to engage meaningfully with reality, to participate well in the ongoing creative advance of the universe becoming conscious of itself.

And that's what understanding is for—not complete answers, but sufficient clarity to live well.

SOURCES AND FURTHER READINGS

This book draws on ideas from multiple philosophical traditions and scientific disciplines. Rather than formal citations, what follows is a guide to sources organized by theme, with brief descriptions of where to explore further. The suggestions emphasize accessible works for general readers, though some more technical sources are included for those who want to go deeper.

ON PROCESS PHILOSOPHY

The core insight that reality is better understood as process than as things has a long history, but its most systematic development came in the twentieth century.

Alfred North Whitehead's *Process and Reality* (1929) is the foundational text, though it's notoriously difficult. Whitehead, a mathematician and philosopher, developed a comprehensive metaphysics where "actual occasions" of experience are fundamental and enduring objects are patterns in process. For more accessible introductions to Whitehead's thought, try

Modes of Thought by Whitehead himself, or secondary sources like *Whitehead's Philosophy* by A. H. Johnson or *Understanding Whitehead* by Victor Lowe.

Charles Hartshorne developed process philosophy in theological directions, but his *Creative Synthesis and Philosophic Method* (1970) offers a clear exposition of core process ideas. David Ray Griffin has written extensively on process thought, including *Unsnarling the World-Knot: Consciousness, Freedom, and the Mind-Body Problem* (1998), which directly addresses the consciousness puzzles this book engages.

For contemporary process philosophy accessible to general readers, Catherine Keller's *Cloud of the Impossible* (2015) combines process thinking with theology and postmodern thought. Arran Gare's *The Philosophical Foundations of Ecological Civilization* (2017) shows how process philosophy addresses contemporary environmental concerns.

ON CONSCIOUSNESS AND EXPERIENCE

The view that experience might be fundamental rather than emergent has ancient roots but contemporary defenders.

Thomas Nagel's "What Is It Like to Be a Bat?" (1974) remains the classic statement of why subjective experience resists purely physical explanation. His *Mind and Cosmos* (2012) argues that consciousness requires rethinking our basic understanding of nature, though his specific proposals differ from those developed here.

David Chalmers's *The Conscious Mind* (1996) introduced the term "hard problem of consciousness" for the explanatory gap between physical processes and felt experience. While Chalmers doesn't fully embrace the view that experience is fundamental, he takes seriously the possibility of panpsychism—the view that consciousness is widespread in nature.

For accessible defenses of panpsychism—the view that experience goes all the way down—see Philip Goff's *Galileo's Error* (2019), which argues that consciousness must be fundamental to solve the combination problem. Galen Strawson's essays, collected in *Real Materialism and Other Essays* (2008), defend "realistic physicalism" where the physical is inherently experiential.

On the neuroscience of consciousness, Anil Seth's *Being You: A New Science of Consciousness* (2021) offers an accessible account of how brains generate experience, though from a more conventional materialist perspective. Antonio Damasio's *The Feeling of What Happens* (1999) explores how consciousness emerges from bodily processes.

ON PHYSICS, RELATIONALITY, AND OBSERVATION

Quantum mechanics reveals that observation affects what's observed and that particles are better understood relationally than as independent entities.

For accessible introductions to quantum mechanics,

try Jim Al-Khalili's *Quantum: A Guide for the Perplexed* (2003) or Carlo Rovelli's *Helgoland* (2021), which emphasizes the relational interpretation. Karen Barad's *Meeting the Universe Halfway* (2007) develops a sophisticated philosophy where matter and meaning emerge through relationships, though it's more academic.

On relativity and the relational nature of space-time, Carlo Rovelli's *The Order of Time* (2018) is beautifully written and philosophically rich. Lee Smolin's *Time Reborn* (2013) argues that time is fundamental and relationality is key to understanding physics.

For the broader implications of modern physics for our understanding of reality, see Heisenberg's *Physics and Philosophy* (1958), which reflects on quantum mechanics' philosophical significance from one of its founders. Bernard d'Espagnat's *On Physics and Philosophy* (2006) explores what physics reveals about the nature of reality.

ON RELATIONALITY AND INTERDEPENDENCE

The insight that things are constituted by their relationships appears in multiple traditions.

In Western philosophy, Martin Buber's *I and Thou* (1923) is a classic on the fundamental nature of relationship. More recently, Karen Barad's work (mentioned above) develops "agential realism" where entities emerge through relationships rather than preceding them.

In biology, Francisco Varela, Humberto Maturana, and Evan Thompson's work on autopoiesis and enactive cognition emphasizes that organisms and environments are mutually constitutive. Thompson's *Mind in Life* (2007) is the best comprehensive treatment, showing how life and mind are essentially relational.

Ecology has long emphasized interdependence. Fritjof Capra's *The Web of Life* (1996) offers an accessible introduction to systems thinking in biology. More recently, Sheldrake's *Entangled Life* (2020) reveals the profound interconnectedness of fungi and ecosystems in vivid, accessible prose.

ON PARTICIPATORY KNOWING

The view that knowing is participatory rather than passive observation appears in multiple forms.

In philosophy of science, Thomas Kuhn's *The Structure of Scientific Revolutions* (1962) showed how scientific paradigms shape what scientists observe. More radical is Paul Feyerabend's *Against Method* (1975), arguing that the scientific method itself is more participatory and creative than usually acknowledged.

Michael Polanyi's *Personal Knowledge* (1958) argues that all knowledge involves tacit, participatory dimensions that can't be fully formalized. His *The Tacit Dimension* (1966) is shorter and more accessible.

In quantum mechanics, John Wheeler's concept of "participatory universe" suggests observation genuinely participates in creating reality. His ideas are discussed in John Archibald Wheeler and Kenneth Ford's *Geons, Black Holes, and Quantum Foam* (1998).

Maurice Merleau-Ponty's phenomenology, especially *Phenomenology of Perception* (1945), emphasizes that perception is active engagement rather than passive reception. His later work *The Visible and the Invisible* (1964) develops ideas about the intertwining of perceiver and perceived.

ON ISLAMIC PHILOSOPHY

While this book doesn't explicitly cite Islamic sources, several insights—particularly about existence, process, and the interpenetration of matter and consciousness—have deep roots in Islamic metaphysics.

Mullā Ṣadrā (d. 1640) developed a comprehensive process-oriented metaphysics where existence is fundamentally active and reality is ongoing becoming. His *The Transcendent Philosophy of the Four Journeys of the Intellect* synthesizes Aristotelian philosophy, Neoplatonism, Islamic theology, and mystical insight. For accessible introductions, see Sajjad Rizvi's *Mullā Ṣadrā and Metaphysics: Modulation of Being* (2009) or Ibrahim Kalin's *Knowledge in Later Islamic Philosophy* (2010).

Ibn 'Arabī (d. 1240) developed a profound metaphysics of divine self-disclosure where reality is ongoing creative manifestation and existence itself is relationship. William Chittick's *The Sufi Path of Knowledge* (1989) offers extensive translations and commentary. For a more accessible overview, see Claude Addas's *Quest for the Red Sulphur: The Life of Ibn 'Arabi* (1993).

More generally on Islamic philosophy, Peter Adamson's *Philosophy in the Islamic World* (2016) provides an accessible historical survey, while Seyyed Hossein Nasr's *Islamic Philosophy from Its Origin to the Present* (2006) emphasizes the living tradition.

ON LIVING WITH THIS UNDERSTANDING

Several contemporary works explore how to live in light of understanding reality as process, relational, and participatory.

Iain McGilchrist's *The Master and His Emissary* (2009) explores how different modes of attention reveal different aspects of reality, with profound implications for how we inhabit the world. His more recent *The Matter with Things* (2021) is encyclopedic and brilliant.

Buddhist philosophy has long emphasized process, interdependence, and the participatory nature of experience. For accessible introductions that connect with contemporary science and philosophy, try Evan Thompson's *Why I Am Not a Buddhist* (2020), which offers a philosophically sophisticated engagement with Buddhist ideas, or B. Alan Wallace's *The Taboo of Subjectivity* (2000), which argues for including contemplative methods in investigating consciousness.

On finding meaning in a naturalistic worldview, see Rebecca Goldstein's *36 Arguments for the Existence of God: A Work of Fiction* (2010), which includes a lucid appendix on philosophical arguments, or Thomas Nagel's *Secular Philosophy and the Religious Temperament* (2010), collected essays on meaning without transcendence.

For practical implications of understanding ourselves as embedded, embodied, and relational, see Andy Clark's *Natural-Born Cyborgs* (2003) on how tools and technologies extend mind, or Alva Noë's *Out of Our Heads* (2009), which argues consciousness isn't locked inside the brain but is enacted through bodily and environmental engagement.